Public Speaking:
A Very Short Course

7 Lessons for the Classroom, for Workshops, or for Individuals

Diane Windingland

Copyright © 2015 by Diane Windingland

All rights reserved. No part of this publication may be reproduced or transmitted in any form or by any means, mechanical or electronic, including photocopying and recording, or by any information storage and retrieval system, without prior written permission of the author, except by a reviewer, who may quote brief passages in review.

Contents

Introduction 4
About the Author 4
   How to Use This Material 5
1. Why Develop Public Speaking Skills? 7
2. Define Your Message 9
3. Plan Your Message Structure 11
4. Engage Your Audience with Stories 13
5. Say It With Style! 17
6. Easy PowerPoint Principles 19
7. Deliver with Confidence 21
Resources 23
   Speech Planning & Outline 23
   Speech evaluation form (for peer evaluation) 24
   Impromptu Speaking 25

Introduction

Public speaking is an essential skill for success, and one that creates a great deal of apprehension for many people. This short course in public speaking will quickly give you, or students you teach, the basics of public speaking in a focused format that is flexible in how you use it. This book is a work-text, intended for readers not just to read, but to write in as concepts are learned and applied. Practice this material and gain confidence in your speaking abilities.

About the Author

Diane Windingland is the author of several books on communication skills including *Cat Got Your Tongue?*, *12 Ways to be a Confident Speaker*, *Public Speaking Lessons from TED Talks* and more. Originally trained as an engineer, she now speaks for organizations that want to help their people have better, more profitable conversations and presentations. She also coaches people on how to create more dynamic and engaging presentations in high stakes communications.

As a member of Toastmasters International, she has achieved the organization's highest educational award for public speaking and leadership, Distinguished Toastmaster.

Diane recommends joining a Toastmaster club as a cost-effective and fun way to develop communication and leadership skills in a peer-led environment. Go to toastmasters.org for more information or to find a club.

Diane's websites: SmallTalkBigResults.com and VirtualSpeechCoach.com
Please contact Diane with ideas, comments and suggestions for improvement. Diane@VirtualSpeechCoach.com

How to Use This Material

Recommended companion book: *Cat Got Your Tongue? Powerful Public Speaking Skills & Presentation Strategies*

Individuals: In a pinch, you could go through this material the night before a short presentation and use it to greatly enhance your presentation. More time is better.

Facilitators for workshops/classrooms: The material can be adapted to a one hour or longer workshop, or for use in the classroom (taking up the entire time of one or more classes, or in 15 minute segments).

Prior to class, read the applicable session and the session notes below. Items with an open circle bullet indicate class flow items. Items with a diamond bullet indicate extension activities for a longer workshop or for additional classroom sessions (the extension activities in bold are the minimally recommended additional sessions, to allow for greater participant practice). Impromptu speaking (see resources) can be added to each session, if time allows.

1. **Why Develop Public Speaking Skills? (15 minutes)**
    - Open with individual reflection on the benefits list (2 minutes)
    - Partner share on the benefits list (5 min)
    - Individual reflection on the vision of the speaker they want to be (2 min)
    - Explain project requirements and deadlines and Q&A (5 minutes)
    - ❖ Extension: personal story from facilitator (or participants)

2. **Define Your Message (15 minutes)**
    - In groups of 3 or 4, complete one or more "Define a Message" examples
    - Individually, work on a personal message on the next page (5 min)
    - Return to groups for each to share their own message (4 min)
    - ❖ Extension (or second 15 minute session): Each participant shares his or her audience/topic/think-feel-do/message. Timing depends on the number of participants (30 seconds to 1 minute suggested).

3. **Plan Your Message Structure (15 minutes)**
    - Using an audience volunteer, go through the steps in planning, asking for audience input as you work with the volunteer. A whiteboard or flip chart or some way to show the audience a visual of the process is helpful.
    - ❖ Extension: After each step with the volunteer, allow time for individuals to do the activity for their own topics
    - ❖ **Extension: Have participants turn in an outline (see resources for an outline)**

Public Speaking: A Very Short Course

- ❖ **Extension (or one or two 15 minute class segments): Each participant shares his or her opening (30 seconds to 1 minute), to include 3Ps: Pep, Promise, Path.**

4. **Engage Your Audience with Stories (15 minutes)**
    - Read the material on the first page of this section out loud to the group (4 min)
    - Participants silently read the example on the next page (3 min)
    - Individual reflection: Ask the participants to think about a personal story, relevant to their topic in which they either learned an important lesson or helped someone else learn a lesson (3 min). Optional: use the story format on p. 15.
    - Partner share (5 min)
    - ❖ **Extension (or one or two 15 minute class segments): Each participant shares his or her story with the class**

5. **Say it with Style (Rhetorical Devices)--optional lesson (15 min)**
    - Select 5 students to each read one of the rhetorical devices out loud
    - Partner discussion: Partners help each other to come up with at least one rhetorical device that each can use

6. **Easy PowerPoint Principles--optional lesson (15 min)**
    - Read this page out loud (2 min)
    - Individual activity to plan a few slides (8 min)
    - Partner sharing of slide ideas (5 min)
    - ❖ Extension: Watch the 8-minute video: http://bit.ly/ezppt

7. **Deliver with Confidence (15 min)**
    - Read points one and two out loud to the group
    - Individual activity on the next page: find individual rate of speech and estimate number of words for a presentation (this will cover point 3 also)
    - Individual activity on same page as the previous activity: keywords
    - Partner sharing of keyword exercise (rule: must look at person when talking)
    - Read points 4 and 5 out loud
    - Review project requirements and participant presentation schedule
    - ❖ **Extension (one or more class segments): each participant presents**
    - ❖ Extension: video of presentation (dress rehearsal, can be done in small groups)
    - ❖ Extension: videos uploaded to an online platform (with permission) for participant use as desired (online portfolio)
    - ❖ Extension: peer evaluations (see resources for an evaluation format)
    - ❖ Extension: competition (judging criteria will vary, participants should be given the criteria and any requirements at the start of this program)

1. Why Develop Public Speaking Skills?

Which benefits of gaining public speaking skills do you want?

I want to be able to:

- Ace the presentation portion of other classes
- Manage the fear of public speaking
- Increase my confidence level in professional and social situations
- Develop critical thinking skills
- Take on leadership roles more easily
- Learn audience-empathy through honing material to meet an audience's needs
- Get the job! Answer job interview questions confidently
- Advance my career--learn skills that are valuable to employers
- Provide project updates clearly and concisely
- Instruct classmates, coworkers or employees in an engaging manner
- Add to my professional credibility/resume through speaking at events/ conferences
- Persuade others to change beliefs, take action or reconsider a decision
- Win presentation contests
- Pitch an idea to secure funding for a startup company
- Become a thought leader
- Become a change agent
- Other reasons: _____

Create a vision of the speaker you want to be. Imagine the best possible version of yourself speaking in front of an audience that you care about on a topic that you are passionate about.

What do you look like? (posture, facial expression, body movement, attire)

How do you sound? (tone, loudness, rate of speech)

How is the audience responding to you and your presentation? (attention, nodding, smiling, thoughtful)

Try drawing it! (use the next page)

Public Speaking: A Very Short Course

For the artistically inclined, try sketching a picture of yourself speaking to your ideal audience (stick figures with happy faces are OK!)

2. Define Your Message

Whether your presentation is one minute or one hour, it should only have one main message. A longer presentation may have more supporting points, but the message should be singular. You should be able to state your point in one sentence. You may never actually use your defining statement exactly as written in your presentation, but your entire presentation should support your main message. When defining your message, begin with the end in mind. At the end of your presentation, what do you want people to think, feel, or do? Consider why your audience would care.

Define a message exercise. In the examples below, the "think, feel, or do" is defined for an audience. Try your hand at writing a one-sentence main message for at least one of the scenarios. I suggest writing your message as a "you" message as if you are speaking to one individual. Then create the "think, feel, do" and message for your audience and topic. *Use the next page to brainstorm and to have more space to write your message.*

Audience	topic	Audience "think, feel, do"	Message in one-sentence
College students	Presentation skills	Think: That they can speak with power and confidence Feel: Excited to present Do: Speak on a topic of high interest at the next class	Learning powerful public speaking skills will give you the confidence to voice your message and to change your world.
Prospective employer	Job interview	Think: That you have technical and social competencies that their company needs Feel: Confident that you will be a good fit for their company Do: Hire you!	
College Professor	Extra credit for a better grade	Think: That allowing an extra credit project opportunity for the class will enhance learning Feel: Both smart and kind Do: Allow an extra credit project	
Boss and Coworkers	Project proposal	Think: That this project will bring much-needed cash flow to the company Feel: Optimistic that the project will be on-time and under-budget Do: Provide assistance with resources (manpower/material)	
Your Audience	Your Topic	Think: Feel: Do:	Your Message

Public Speaking: A Very Short Course

Exercise: Define a message brainstorming

Your Audience:

- Who are they?
- Age range?
- Male to female ratio?
- Job responsibilities?
- Biggest pain points?
- Why would they care?
- What do they expect? (are there elements that are expected or required)

Your topic (combine your personal and professional experience as well as your passion, consider profitability, if applicable):

Think-feel-do:

- What do you want your audience to think after your presentation?

- What do you want your audience to feel after your presentation?

- What do you want your audience to do after your presentation?

Your message (a one-sentence, audience-focused message, written as if you are speaking to an individual):

3. Plan Your Message Structure

A well-organized presentation can draw your audience in and take them on a journey to a destination you choose and it also can help you remember what you want to say!

1. Begin with your message statement and what you want your audience to think, feel, or do after your presentation. You may need to do some initial brainstorming (step 3).

2. Decide on the type of structure that will most effectively accomplish #1:
   - **Basic (similar to a 5 paragraph essay)**: introduction of thesis, 3 supporting points, conclusion (summarize, call-to-action)
   - **Short presentation structure: PREP** (State your **P**oint, give a **R**eason, provide **E**vidence or an example, restate your **P**oint. PREP can also be used for body points)
   - **Problem-Cause-Solution** (an effective variation for persuasive speeches is the Then-Now-How variation: using a specific case, show the past condition, the improved present condition, and then explain how your process, product or idea is the "how")
   - **Chronological or Spatial** (First, second, third, or then, now, tomorrow, or by location)
   - **Story-based.** A story can be used in all of the above structures, but can also be the basis for a presentation (more on story in the next session topic)

3. Brainstorm some ideas--use mind-mapping, whiteboards, post-it notes, index cards or plain paper. Bounce ideas off others. The goal is to have more ideas than you can use.

4. Decide on your key points (must all support your main message). For all but the shortest speeches, 3 key points is a time-tested number that works well for you and your audience to remember. A very short speech of 2-3 minutes only needs one key point.

5. Decide on the supporting content (the mental anchors) of your key points. The acronym **SHARP** can help you remember the most common types of anchors: **S**tory (or analogy or metaphor), **H**umor, **A**ctivity (audience activity or demonstration), **R**eference (quote, research, evidence), **P**hoto/prop (includes presentation software)

6. Craft your introduction and conclusion.
   Intro: 3 Ps: Pep, Promise, Path. Begin with a little pep, and get their attention with a story, a startling statement, or a quote. Then promise a benefit to the audience (how will what you are about to tell them make their lives better?). Finally give your audience the path of your presentation and preview your points

   Conclusion: Revisit your points, close with a big anchor, have a call-to-action.
   Plan your presentation and create an outline on the next page

Public Speaking: A Very Short Course

Exercise: Speech Planning & Outline

Who is my audience?

Why will they care?

What do I want my audience to think, feel, or do after my presentation?

Main Message (one sentence):

Introduction:

    Pep (attention):

    Promise (benefit to audience):

    Path (preview of points):

Transition to body:

Body:

    Key Point 1:

    Support (SHARP: Story, Humor, Activity, Reference, Photo/prop):

    Transition to next point:

    Key Point 2:

    Support (SHARP: Story, Humor, Activity, Reference, Photo/prop):

    Transition to next point:

    Key Point 3:

    Support (SHARP: Story, Humor, Activity, Reference, Photo/prop):

    Transition to conclusion:

Conclusion: Revisit your points, close with a big anchor, have a call-to-action.

4. Engage Your Audience with Stories

Stories touch our emotions and linger in our minds. If you want your audience to remember your points, or you want to persuade, use stories. Facts tell, but stories sell. Use the following tips to create engaging stories:

1. **The story must be relevant to your point.** Don't tell a story just to tell a story.

2. **There must be conflict.** A story is usually only interesting if there is some sort of conflict (conflict types: person vs. person, person vs. self, person vs. nature, person vs. society, person vs. technology). Get to the conflict as quickly as possible. Provide just enough background/context to make the story relevant or understandable.

Here is the standard "Hero Story" format:

(Main character)_____ is in (circumstances/setting)_____ and needs to (Goal)_____ but faces _____(obstacles/opponents) when_____ (Climax/conflict occurs, often more than once) until _____ (resolution--obstacles or opponents are overcome)

3. **Use a little bit of drama**
   a) **The dramatic pause.** Pause a couple of seconds before and after a climatic situation or phrase to heighten the anticipation. "To be or not to be?" (pause, pause), "That is the question."
   b) **Dialogue.** Don't just narrate. Use narration to set up dialogue (characters talking to each other). Dialogue is the heart of an engaging story.
   c) **Act it out.** Let your facial expressions convey emotions. Get your body into the story. Don't just say, "We pushed the car out of the ditch," but actually act out at least the hand gesture of pushing.

Where can you get ideas for stories?

Your personal experiences. (should be the primary source for your stories). As related to your topic, what experiences have given you "aha" moments, moments that changed what you thought, felt, or did? Use photos, journals and other records to jog your memory.

Second-degree experiences. Second-degree experiences are ones in which someone told you about their experiences (lessons from your grandmother's life, a client's story or testimonial).

Other sources. You may have read or heard a story that is relevant to your presentation. If you use a story other than your own, you need to attribute the source.

Example: Tell Your Story

1. Know your point! What is the relevant point of the story? (*Example point: Champion the Underdog. My grandmother modeled standing up for people*)

2. Paint a picture (without dragging on, providing just enough detail to provide context) Example set up: *It was Christmas Eve, 1968. I was six years old and I still believed in Santa. We had just arrived at a family Christmas party--my mother's side of the family, all good Italian Catholics, with big families. Santa Claus was handing out gifts, calling out each child's name...*

3. Get them in the gut (What created feelings of Joy, Sadness, Fear, Anger or Frustration?)

4. Use a story structure (The points are indicated for the example story that follows):
    1. Main character : 6 year old Diane
    2. inciting event (a problem): Diane didn't get a gift from Santa
    3. What happened leading to the climax: Grandma intervened
    4. Climax/Turning point: Santa gave Diane an awesome gift
    5. Resolution/solution: Diane learned an important lesson from Grandma

As it got closer and closer to my turn, I squeezed my grandmother's hand. Finally, it was the last gift. My gift. Santa Claus raised it up high, and called out, "Ho, ho, ho, Theresa Coffee." (reaction) What?? I felt like I'd been sucker punched. Has that ever happened to you? Has someone else ever got something you deserved? Like a promotion or a job? Well that's how I felt. After I recovered from the shock, tears welled up and I looked up at my nana, my big Italian grandma, and said, "Santa forgot me!" My nana scooped me up in those fleshy arms, arms that every morning rolled out ravioli at an Italian restaurant, and said, "Oh no, Santa did not forget you!" And she passed me off to my parents who tried to shield me from what grandma was doing, but I saw her work the crowd and I saw her get her younger brothers, my great uncles, to work the crowd too. Well, a few minutes later, a sheepish-looking Santa Claus approached me. "Little Diane Williams, I'm sorry. Your gift was stuck at the bottom of my bag." And with a flourish, he pulled out a wad of bills. Fifty bucks! A small fortune to a six year old in 1968. My tears vanished and I looked over at my nana. She was smiling like a Cheshire Cat. My grandmother taught me a couple of important lessons that day. The first was that it pays to have ... mafia connections. Well it does pay to have influential people in your life. But the more important lesson was to be a champion for the underdog.

Exercise: Tell Your Story, Your Turn!

1. Know your point! What is the relevant point of the story?

2. Paint a picture (without dragging on, providing just enough detail to provide context)

3. Get them in the gut (What created feelings of Joy, Sadness, Fear, Anger or Frustration?)
(Relate to the audience's pain, if possible)

4. Use a story structure
   - Main character (can be a client or customer) :

   - inciting event (a problem):

   - What happened leading to the climax:

   - Climax/Turning point:

   - Resolution/solution:

5. Practice and revise

Additional Story Notes:

5. Say It With Style!

Create mental anchors with rhetorical devices

SCREAM to Give Your Presentations Power!*

Simile—using "like" or "as" to compare

>He screamed like a little girl. He hid under the table, as quiet as a mouse.

Contrast—pairing of opposites

>Churchill: There is only one answer to <u>defeat</u> and that is <u>victory</u>. (It's a bonus if you can also use alliteration. For example: From the depths of <u>tragedy</u>, he rose to <u>triumph</u>)

Some opposite pairs: Present—Past (or Future), Beginning—End, Dark—Light, Friend—Foe.

Rhyme

Benjamin Franklin: An apple a <u>day</u> keeps the doctor <u>away</u>.

Echo: Repetition of a word or phrase

Churchill: <u>We shall fight</u> on the beaches, <u>we shall fight</u> on the landing grounds, <u>we shall fight</u> in the streets, <u>we shall fight</u> in the hiss; <u>we shall</u> never surrender.

Alliteration—repetition of the beginning sounds of a word.

>Martin Luther King, Jr.: I have a dream that my little children will one day live in a nation where they will be judged not by the <u>c</u>olor of their skin but by the <u>c</u>ontent of their <u>c</u>haracter.

Metaphor—directly says that something is something else.

>His beard was a lion's mane.
>
>Bullets of hate shot from his mouth.
>
>His bark is worse than his bite.

*The SCREAM structure was coined in 2005 by Dr. Randy J. Harvey, the 2004 World Champion of Public Speaking and has been taught around the globe since then.

Public Speaking: A Very Short Course

Exercise: Rhetorical Devices (pick one or more to add punch to your presentation):

Simile: Is there an analogy you can use? Is an unfamiliar concept like something more familiar?

Your turn:

Contrast: What are ideas you can contrast? Can you use contrast to structure your points? (Before/After) If you need some ideas on opposite pairings, check out Thesaurus.com

Your turn:

Rhyme

For example, someone speaking about moving around to stay healthy could boil the message down to: *Be fit. Don't sit.* If you need help with ideas for rhymes, look online!

- Try using synonyms to explore words at Thesaurus.com.
- Use a rhyming dictionary, such as Rhymezone.com

Your turn:

Echo:

Beginning phrases with the same word: *My kind of party: Good food. Good friends. Good fun.*

Ending phrases with the same word (or phrase): *When I was a child I talked like a child, I thought like a child, I reasoned like a child. (I Corinthians 13:11)*

Your turn:

Alliteration:

Try creating your own phrases, which will be as memorable as clichés: *Sink or swim,* or a *dime a dozen.* Don't go overboard in using alliteration.

Your turn:

Metaphor (compare two things without using like)

A common example when people talk about needing to take care of yourself before taking care of others: *Put on your own oxygen mask first.*

Your turn:

6. Easy PowerPoint Principles

PowerPoint, or other presentation software can enhance a presentation if used well. Unfortunately, it usually isn't! Create an elegant and simple PowerPoint by following these 4 easy tips:

1. **Plan outside of PowerPoint.** Don't start presentation planning in PowerPoint, but create a presentation that you could give without PowerPoint (especially useful if the technology fails), and then consider how you can enhance your presentation with the visual support of presentation software. Try planning on sticky notes that can be easily rearranged, and then transfer your sticky note outline to PowerPoint slides.

   Sticky note planning example:

2. **Use less text and more pictures.**
   Fewer words can help people understand more by reducing complexity. Personally I try not to use more text or bullets than dictated the 6X6 rule: No more than 6 bullets with no more than 6 words per bullet, with only 6 lines (no wrapping). Usually, I prefer much, much less text than even that. Pictures and simple graphical representation of data are much easier to understand

3. **Use BIG pictures for a BIG impact** (let the picture take up the whole slide, if possible)

4. **Proof-read and then practice your presentation several times** (don't read the slides!). Have a hard-copy outline to keep you on track, especially if the technology fails.

   For an 8-minute video of PowerPoint tips: http://bit.ly/ezppt

Public Speaking: A Very Short Course

Exercise: Plan your Power Point

Using your outline, consider how you could visually support your presentation. Use the boxes below or sticky notes:

7. Deliver with Confidence

You have a singular, compelling message that flows logically. You have written out your presentation. How do you go from a written speech to a speech performance?

1. **Write out your speech conversationally** (Write for the ear, not the eye). If you compare a speech to an essay, a speech will have shorter sentences, shorter words, contractions ("I'm" instead of "I am") and will address the listener directly (using phrases that start with "If you do . . ." instead of "If one does . . .")

2. **Meet the time requirement.** If you know your rate of speech (words per minute), you can roughly estimate how many words you need to have in your speech. My normal speaking rate is about 140 words per minute, so if I want a 3 minute speech, it would need to be about 420 words long (3 min X 140 wpm). You can estimate your rate of speech by timing yourself as you conversationally read something you wrote (divide the number of words by the number of minutes). *Exercise on next page*

3. **Reduce your speech to key word notes. Practice.** (Keywords: no more than about 3 words per sentence, plus any non-word symbols). Remember your goal in eye contact: Talk to people, not to paper. Practice from your keywords or outline in a way that forces you to make eye contact (you can put up a few sheets of paper with crudely drawn faces to simulate audiences members). Look down at your keywords (but don't talk while looking down), speak while looking at your "audience." Look at Audience. Speak. Stop Speaking. Look down. Look up. Speak. Repeat. Reduce your notes until you either don't need them at all, or you only have the concepts (or specific figures or quotes) written down. *Exercise on next page*

4. **Conduct a dress-rehearsal,** simulating your presentation conditions as closely as possible (extremely important if using presentation software or props). If you can get a live audience to attend your dress rehearsal, you will get valuable audience experience that can give you a great deal of confidence. You can also video yourself and self-evaluate your performance. Create a checklist of items needed for your presentation.

5. **Prepare for success.** Prepare physically with targeted practice, rehearsal and revision. Also, plan for the first impression you will make: your clothes (generally, you make a better first impression by dressing one-level better than your audience), your approach to the speaking area, shaking the hand of the emcee, smiling at your audience, etc. Prepare mentally by envisioning a successful picture of yourself giving your presentation. Tell yourself, "I'm excited!" not, "I'm nervous." Tell yourself that you are giving the audience a gift. Be excited to give them that gift.

Public Speaking: A Very Short Course

Exercises: Estimate your individual rate of speech and the number of words for a presentation (you can use your cell phone to time and calculate).

1. Time how long it takes to read point number 3 on the previous page (keyword notes) TWICE (240 words if read twice) at a CONVERSATIONAL rate.

   Time (to read twice): _____

2. Estimate your personal rate of speech (For example, if it takes a person 104 seconds to read the paragraph TWICE, the calculation is 240 words divided by 104 seconds, times 60 seconds/min = 138 wpm)

   240 words divided by your time _____ X 60 seconds/min = _____ wpm

3. Estimate how many words your presentation needs to be.
   Using the example rate of 138 wpm, if the planned presentation is 3 minutes, then the approximate word count is 3 min X 138 wpm = 414 words.

   Length of presentation in minutes _____ X your wpm _____ = _____ words

Practice reducing to keywords (reduce each sentence below to keywords, then deliver from keywords only, remembering to look up when speaking)

1. (Keywords: no more than about 3 words per sentence, plus any non-word symbols).
2. Remember your goal in eye contact: Talk to people, not to paper.
3. Practice from your keywords or outline in a way that forces you to make eye contact (you can put up a few sheets of paper with crudely drawn faces to simulate audiences members).
4. Look down at your keywords (but don't talk while looking down), speak while looking at your "audience."
5. Look at Audience. Speak. Stop Speaking. Look down. Look up. Speak. Repeat.
6. Reduce your notes until you either don't need them at all, or you only have the concepts (or specific figures or quotes) written down.

Your keywords from above:

1. _____, _____, _____
2. _____, _____, _____
3. _____, _____, _____
4. _____, _____, _____
5. _____, _____, _____
6. _____, _____, _____

Resources

Speech Planning & Outline

Who is my audience?

Why will they care?

What do I want my audience to think, feel, or do after my presentation?

Main Message (one sentence):

Introduction:

    Pep (attention):

    Promise (benefit to audience):

    Path (preview of points):

Transition to body:

Body:

    Key Point 1:

    Support (SHARP: Story, Humor, Activity, Reference, Photo/prop):

    Transition to next point:

    Key Point 2:

    Support (SHARP: Story, Humor, Activity, Reference, Photo/prop):

    Transition to next point:

    Key Point 3:

    Support (SHARP: Story, Humor, Activity, Reference, Photo/prop):

    Transition to conclusion:

Conclusion: Revisit your points, close with a big anchor, have a call-to-action.

Speech evaluation form (for peer evaluation)

Outline	Items to consider	Notes:

	Organization
	
	✓ Clear beginning, middle, end
	✓ Opening grabs attention
	✓ Body
	    o A few main points
	    o Points supported
	    o Engaging story
	✓ Good transitions
	✓ Close—strong (summary, call for action)	

	Delivery ✓ Physical appearance ✓ Manner (confident, enthusiastic) ✓ Vocal variety, Pacing ✓ Word choice ✓ Eye contact ✓ Any distracting mannerisms? ✓ Use of gestures ✓ Body Language ✓ Dialogue in story ✓ Use of props	
	Purpose ✓ Did the speaker help you care about the topic? ✓ Did the speaker keep your attention? ✓ Do you think, feel or want to act differently?	

The best part was:

Impromptu Speaking

Most of the speaking you do is not prepared presentations, but impromptu. Someone asks you a question and you have to respond. Sometimes your response is in a high-stakes situation, such as a job interview, or in a Q&A session in which you are pitching a business idea or selling something. Practice now! Practicing impromptu speaking can improve your ability to speak off the top of your head without losing your mind!

One easy format to follow is the short presentation structure PREP (State your **P**oint, give a **R**eason, provide **E**vidence or an example, restate your **P**oint).

In a class situation, if time allows, a few minutes of each session can be dedicated to impromptu speaking, with one of the participants acting as the "Impromptu Leader" for the day, posing questions to a few other fellow participants (I suggest the facilitator offer a theme, and conduct the first session of impromptu speaking as an example to follow).

The format is something like this:

1. Impromptu Leader briefly introduces the theme

2. Impromptu Leader asks the first question (not too complicated, and not a "yes" or "no" question) and then calls on a participant (this let everyone wonder if they will have to respond to the question and keeps people on their toes).

3. Participant 1 answers in a pre-determined time (30 seconds to 1 minute, or 1 to 2 minutes). Time the response and indicate at least the minimum and maximum times (can used colored folders). An example for a 1-2 minute topic: 1 minute (green), 1.5 min (Yellow), 2 min (Red).

4. Impromptu Leader optionally makes a transition comment and then asks the second question and calls on another participant.

5. The Impromptu Leader calls on as many participants as time allows.

See the next page for use in making an "Impromptu Leader" assignment

Public Speaking: A Very Short Course

Impromptu Leader Assignment

Impromptu Leader: Prior to class, the Impromptu Leader will do 3 things: select a theme, prepare questions related to the theme and prepare a 1-2 minute talk to introduce the theme. During class, after introducing the theme, the Impromptu Leader will state a question and then call randomly on impromptu participants to respond for 1-2 minutes, until the allotted time is used Each impromptu participant should have a different question.

Theme:

1-2 minute talk to introduce theme (Key points):

List of Questions: